Memoirs Of A Lyric

Maroon Shade

BookLeaf Publishing

India | USA | UK

Made with ❤ on the BookLeaf Publishing Platform
www.bookleafpub.in
www.bookleafpub.com

Dedication

To the lover in you...

Preface

Passionate words with a musical flair inspired by God,
life and love.

Acknowledgements

Let's Begin

Welcome to the inside of my head.

Hope you enjoy the ride.

Like a rollercoaster sometimes.

But you might gain perspective in the highs.

I invite you to have an open mind.

We all take time to grow.

Without further ado

Enjoy the show!

Music

I wake up thinking of you,
Just wondering where you are.
Making sure you were right where I left you.
The first thing I think about
When I leave the house.
The last thing I think about
Before I go to sleep.
I'm obsessed with you.
Whenever I don't have you,
I'm not happy!
I need your melody, rhythm, soul.
The joy you bring me
When I listen to you!
The different personalities you have,
All of them I respect and love!
I'm in love with the notes, many voices, beats.
They make my emotions more profound!
Making every emotion deeper felt!
Like nothing else ever has!
I love my musical soul, spirit, life!

Iloveyou

I can give my emotions to other guys,
But you are the only one that keeps my heart.
From now to forever my loyalty is only to you,
My heart, body and soul only wants you.
Since the moment I saw you,
No other man mattered.
Everything stopped and all I could see was you.
For days I waited to hear your voice,
Hear your laugh.
Fell in love with you before I met you,
Haven't been able to fall out.
Sometimes I want to because it's like you don't see me.
You don't see how I try to be closer to you when I see
you,
How my spirit drops when my friends pull me away.
Maybe one day you'll notice how deeply I admire you,
Want to just be with you.
But until then I can keep quiet.
Act like what I feel for you is just a crush,

When in reality,
I think I love you! ♥

No One Comes Close

I cant even stand the thought of you.
Just seeing you breaks my heart.
I wanna cry because of all that we went through.
I cant explain how much I miss you.
Cant someone tell me why it hurts SO bad!
I cant stand being near you because it hurts so much,
You never took me seriously.
Just saying it I can breath again,
But I'm paralyzed when I remember the kiss, the hugs.
Then the hurt

Fallen Angel

The gates of heaven part
And out of the rain of the world
Comes you, shiny and new, and beautiful.
So I show you my world
Bring joy to your eyes
As something different intrigues you.
Sometimes you soul is too high up to touch.
So I wanna bring you down
To my level and show you how I feel.
You did come down one deep dark day,
And brought me so much joy.
So I wanted you to stay.
The longer you stayed with me in your arms
I noticed a change.
Something took away your charms.
The gleam in your eyes turned into a flame.
I couldn't help but to think that I was to blame.
I was selfish, greedy, how could I not see it.
I took the beautiful angel you were and changed you.
I told you everything and sent you back to your

hometown,
In heaven where you belong.
But before you left, that same smile,
That gleam in your eye came back.
I will forever miss my fallen angel.
Till we meet again...

Whenever

Keep my heart with you wherever you go,
I gave it to you for a reason.
Hold it close when you really need it.
Put it away when you don't.
But always keep it near you,
Cuz I feel like you'll have a hard life without it.
In a perfect world you're my husband,
And we have four kids deciding on five.
But since that's kinda impossible,
Take my hopes and dreams with you.
And make them true for someone else.
Cuz obviously, God doesn't want us together.
Not now anyway.
Maybe it's just bad timing,
Or were too different.
Just want you to know,
That wherever you go,
You'll always carry my heart.
Give it back when you need me.
And take it whenever you get lonely.

Just know my love and respect is unconditional.
Forever and always.

Unrequainted

My heart belongs to you
In whatever shape or format you present yourself.
I hate the inability to control myself around you.
I finally admit that I love you to myself,
And maybe it got a little easier,
I dont know yet.
I cant breath when I see you with someone else,
Even though you were never mine.
You were Never mine.
I see you with her and to me you don't seem happy,
Neither does she.
Maybe that's what you want,
Something to keep you miserable.
So you don't have to get hurt
If love actually came to you.
I love you,
But as long as you'll be with her,
You'll never know.
I wish things were simple and I could make myself feel
this way about someone else.

Love will get uncontrollable if you don't keep an eye on reality.

Soon I won't have to see you ever again!

I might be able to move on and actually fall in love.

The Nearness of You

The love of my life is unattainable.
Always has been since the first time I said, "Hey."
I keep a spot in my heart open to you,
So if you ever step out of your perfect life,
You know you always have a home here with me.
You make my grass a little greener,
My songs more like poetry.
When I'm around you it's hard not to smile.
Brought me to a higher understanding of love,
Better than anyone else ever has.
It's just the nearness of you.
No one has ever made me feel the way that you have.
And I hope one day to return the favor,
But that'll probably never happen because,
The love of my life is unattainable.

Studio Session

Make passionate music with me
I know you want to.
Take notes from my lips,
The tempo from my hips.
Take me...
Fell the beat bangin through me.
Don't fight the rhythm.
Take me.
We can make melodies.
Blend our harmonies.
Just Take me.
I'm dying to hear your song.
I wanna memorize every lyric.
I can staff a staccato I promise.
My treble clef was meant for your bass.
Just press record.

Act 2

If the wind outside wasn't enough of a sign,
There goes my gut.
The chill in the air feels like it's sharing my luck.
Or changing it...
The rain clouds scared the birds away,
So now I sing alone.
They blocked out the sun,
Stealing away my glow.
Gravity of new earth is a lot stronger.
Air a lot thicker.
Nights a lot colder.
Revealing all of the bits and pieces of myself that I hid
away.
The fight between new and old started to resemble
healthy and toxic.
Becoming necessary for survival.
New days transforming my future self and potential.
I was built to weather the storm because I created it.
May Jesus lead me into a bigger, brighter day.

Vision

I can't stop thinking of the way you blush.
And it takes a lot.
I'm realizing that the light in this room is so much
brighter...
When you're here.
In the breeze is peppered bubbles of your scent.
They evaporate before me bringing memories of joy.
Although my stomach and my cheeks ache,
there's no better way to pass the time.
I believe you're not made from carbon like everyone else.
Maybe gold, covered in diamonds, with a big fire burning
inside.
It's impossible to feel small next to you.
With you I always feel like I'm looking over a mountain.
When you speak,
I hear riffs and ballads with the most beautiful notes.
The way your heart embraces everyone you meet,
there's gotta be more than 4 chambers.
My admiration knows no bounds,

Because your appeal is limitless.
If only the stars knew you.

Lost

The double-edged sword never comes with instructions,
But usually a teacher.
Someone to walk you through it,
Protecting you along the way.
For the warriors who didn't have that,
We struggled.
Women reach for strong principles and actions rather
than trust in words because they've been lied to.
And a lot of men run to chaotic situationships and wild
attitudes because their love was returned empty.
Walls and aggression overcame the need to be seen.
Nonchalance and suppression became more important
than the need to speak.
None choosing better or healthier,
Just reversing the roles in an effort to feel safer.
When in reality we only lost who we were.
Who we are.

True Love

It's so quiet at night.
Hard to sleep when it's this cold.
The stars really are more beautiful,
When I'm watching them with someone.
I've never felt so exposed and ignored at the same time.
The deep pit I dug myself out of is looking real
comfortable right now.
At least I always have me.
Don't ask me what's wrong,
I'm trying to function.
Don't be too kind,
Than I don't feel like you're up to something.
Please leave me alone.
This is where I'm safe.
Not talking.
Not feeling.
Not healing.
Not living.

Well maybe your love might distract me.

I guess it won't hurt to try to be happy.

God, you won!

I'll live again.

Thank you!

Tunnel

Today the sun just feels so bright.
One more hour please.
It's so early to start the day.
Why is it so hard to bend my knees?
But it's another day,
Just keep going,
Get through it.
Like Shia said,
Just do it.
My laugh is gone though.
Not much is funny these days.
I smile in public to keep the questions away.
Let the feelings rot inside.
They never need to see the light of day.
I dont even wanna feel them.
I wish in time they would dissipate.
But instead they only grow and spread all throughout.
And take more of my joy.
Why can't I figure this out?
What am I missing?

Why is it men I keep putting my faith in?
Where did all of my confidence go?
Why is there so much about me I don't know?
Guess it time to face it.
Can no longer weasel around it.
It's time for me to heal.
No how to go about it?

Healing

To be in the presence of God is overwhelming.
In the best possible way.
More intense when you're healing, than on a peaceful
day.
The Lord told me to surrender everything.
But I didn't want to give up the ring.
My hopes for the future.
Not realizing all of that was planned out.
All I had to do was sit down.
And breath.
Be still...
Because God always fulfills!!
He'll teach you the role you're meant to play along the
way.

The Way We're Not

I always loved a good bass slap!
And 808s, boom baps.
They always made me feel alive.
I didn't realize that they dogged me out.
Had me thinking I was nothing without
Your validation,
Attention,
Criticism,
Abuse.
I used to think that was cute.
And then we turned into that too.
Gave men the same poison that they spew.
Now music is no longer about
Originality,
Talent,
Hard work.
Now it resembles who can hurt who the worst.
Then we wonder why we're lost.
Less marriages, less trust.
More violence, less us.

Matching pain for pain so the trauma never goes away.
Somebody tell them we weren't made that way.

24

Pattern

It wasn't really that deep.
You honestly never had to lie to me.
I should've walked away earlier.
But unfulfilled promises and unkempt words made me
stay to see it through.
Will he keep his word today?
Maybe he just forgot?
But a man who is invested will not delay.
He wouldn't let anything or anyone get in his way.
So now I know what it is.
And because you were too kind to just say no,
I'll just do you a favor and leave you alone.
There is no comfort for me here.
My safe space was inside of me all along.
And I done told God how you played me through my
tears.
So prepare yourself.
I wish you the best.

Innerstand

Giving myself time to recognize me.
Having eyes , a beautiful dark brown,
They bring warm, fuzzy feelings.
The lines in my forehead when animated, make me feel
like God drew me for an incredible story.
The inspiration for me must've been magnificent.
My smile truly changes the atmosphere, bringing higher
dimensions of joy and peace.
The way I walk vibrates multitudes of possibilities to
everyone I pass.
My laugh while boisterous can be contagious, spreading
hope for better.
Yes, it will get better.
My calm demeanor invites you to be yourself.
I respect your journey, no matter how different from
mine.
Love is not just a language for me.
It's the way I breath, speak, live.
Yes, I can shut down when I'm bubbled over with
emotions.

Or when I see that the motive is malicious.
Even then I'll still pray for you.
God is never far from me,
Or you.

Faith

The winds picked up again.
Soon the rain will come.
Snow, hail, sleet.
Fire and ice.
Everything under and above the sun.
The sun can stop shining,
The moon can stop glowing.
I will remain calm in the storm,
Because my anchor is the Lord.
Others run, scream and shout.
Fight, argue, as if all is lost.
There's always more to gain,
Within His love.
Always renewed by the second and the day.
Although the world is run by fear,
I will rejoice knowing God made us without fear.
With grace.
With strength.
With love.
He wants to see our big and small moments more than a

truest loved one.

God is so proud of you.

Know that the storm only breaks us down to build us up
into His image.

The Truth

There's a psalm for every struggle that you could be in
the middle of.
There's a story to understand every situation that has
happened in your life.
There is nothing new under the sun.
God hears all your prayers spoken and thought.
He is in all of your moments public and private.
He has been with you this whole time.
Ready to embrace you, when you're ready.
He loves you!

If I Die Today

If I die today,
Know that I cared.
Know that all I've ever wanted was to be there,
For you.
You never had to work hard for my trust.
Even if I never met you, you always had my love.
My respect.

If I die today,
I wasn't in pain.
There's so much faith in my heart,
That God won't do that to me.
And when I pass,
My heart will finally be free.
To love whoever it wants.
And my soul will be full of music!

If I die today,
If anything I'll be relieved to be in the Lord's hands.
I have been in love, won a race,

Saw the future I wanted to make,
For my children.

If I die today,
I wanna make sure I say,
Iloveyou, unconditionally!

www.ingramcontent.com/pod-product-compliance
Lightning Source LLC
Chambersburg PA
CBHW071234140726
47996CB00007B/2602